The Art of German Cooking and Baking

By

Susan R. Huffman

CHAPTER 1.
SOUPS.

No.1—BOUILLON.

4 lbs. ox bones
6 qts. water
⅛ of an onion
½ of a carrot
1 small piece celery
1 small piece kohlrabi
1 small piece parsley root
1 tomato, salt

Preparation: The soup bone is put over the fire in 6 qts. of cold water after it has been washed in cold water. Soup greens and salt are added and the whole is boiled slowly 4 hours until it is boiled down to 2 or 3 quarts. Before using pour the bouillon through a fine sieve. If you like the bouillon very strong and of a good color add ½ teaspoonful of beef extract.

No.2—BOUILLON.

The soup bone and the soup greens are fried light brown with a piece of butter or lard. Water is then added and salt. Boil 4 hours as in the preceding recipe and strain before using.

No.3—OXT AILBOUILLON.

3 lbs. ox-tall
1 tbsp. butter
5 qts. cold water

Salt
Soup greens

Preparation: Cut the ox-tail into small pieces and together with the soup greens, fry them in butter light brown. Add 5 qts. of water and salt. Let it boil 4 or 5 hours slowly down to 2 qts. This bouillon will be very strong and may be served in cups, and bread or cheese sticks may be served with it.

No.4—BOUILLONOFMEA TEXTRACT.

Soup greens
1 tbsp. butter or lard
1 tsp. extract of meat
Salt, 1 qt. water

Preparation: Stew the soup greens in butter or lard a little while, then add water and salt and boil slowly for 20 minutes. Add the meat extract and strain. The yolk of one egg may be stirred into it.

No.5—BOUILLONOFBEEF .

3 lbs. of beef
1 lb. of soup bone
Salt
4 qts. water
Soup greens

Preparation: Soup bone, soup greens, and salt and water are put over the fire to boil one hour, then the beef is addedand the whole is boiled slowly for another 2 or 2½ hours. Strain after boiling. This soup is very strong. Boiled in this way the meat is tender and nourishing.

No.6—BOUILLON.

MadeofRoastBonesorMeatRemnants.

2 lbs. of roast bones
Soup greens
Salt
2 qts. water

Preparation: Chop the bones and put over the fire with soup greens, salt and water; boil 2 hours, then strain. If the bouillon is not strong enough, add a little meat extract.

No.7—DUMPLINGSFORBOUILLON.

MarrowDumplingSoup.

Quantity for 6 Persons.

3 tbsps. of melted beef marrow
2 eggs
¾ pt. grated rolls
½ tsp. chopped parsley
1 pinch nutmeg
1 tbsp. cold water
½ tsp. salt

Preparation: Boil or cook the marrow until it is melted, strain it through a fine sieve. Put 3 tablespoonfuls into a dish and let it cool off. Then beat it to foam and add the yolks of the eggs, salt, parsley, nutmeg, the grated rolls and water. Finally beat the whites of 2 eggs to stiff froth and stir into the mass.

Form small dumplings, let bouillon come to a boil, put the dumplings in and boil slowly ¼ hour.

It is best to try one dumpling first; in case it does not hold together, add some more grated roll.

The soup must be served at once. A little chopped parsley put into it is a pleasing and palatable addition.

No.8—BUTTER-DUMPLINGSOUP .

Quantity for 6 Persons.

2 tbsps. of butter, 2 eggs
¾ pt. grated rolls
¼ tsp. of salt
½ tsp. parsley
1 pinch nutmeg
1 tbsp. of cold water

Preparation of butter-dumplings is the same as the marrow dumplings in No. 7.

The butter is beaten to a cream at once and less salt is added, because the butter is already salted.

No.9—LIVER-DUMPLINGSOUP .

Quantity for 6 Persons.

¼ lb. of chopped calf's liver
1 tsp. butter
A little grated onion
1 tsp. finely chopped parsley
5 tbsps. grated rolls
2 eggs
1 tsp. salt, (scant)
1 pinch nutmeg

Preparation: The butter is stirred and liver, yolk of eggs, salt, parsley, onion, nutmeg and roll crumbs added. The whites of eggs are beaten to a froth and stirred into the mass, then small dumplings are formed. When the bouillon comes to a boil, put the dumplings in and boil ¼ hour.

The soup should be served at once.

No.10—MEA T-DUMPLINGSOUP.

Quantity for 6 Persons.

¼ lb. of finely chopped veal or poultry
2 eggs
¼ pt. grated rolls
1 tsp. of butter
½ tsp. finely chopped parsley
1 tsp. salt
1 pinch nutmeg

Preparation: The butter is stirred, then meat, yolk of eggs, parsley, salt, nutmeg added and well mixed. The whites of eggs beaten to a froth and added to the mass. Small dumplings are formed and when bouillon boils, let the dumplings boil in it 10 minutes. A little parsley may be put into the soup, which must be served at once.

No.1 1—SPONGE-DUMPLINGSOUP.

Quantity for 6 Persons.

3 eggs
¼ tsp. of salt
½ pt. milk or bouillon

Preparation: Eggs and milk or bouillon are well stirred or beaten, salt is added and the mass boiled in double boiler for 20 minutes. If you have no double boiler put your soup into a small pot and place this into a larger one with boiling water.

The bouillon is put into the soup tureen and the dumplings are cut with a teaspoon and put into the bouillon. A little finely chopped parsley is added.

No.12—F ARINA-DUMPLINGSOUP.

Quantity for 6 Persons.

½ pt. milk
4 tbsps. fine farina
1 egg
1 tsp. of butter
¼ tsp. of salt
1 pinch of nutmeg

Preparation: The milk is brought to a boil, stir in the farina and butter and salt, then boil 2 or 3 minutes, stirring constantly until the mass loosens from the pot. Take from the stove, stir into it the yolk of egg. Beat the white of the egg to a froth and add to the mass. When it is cool make small dumplings, or you may also cut into sponges with teaspoon. Let the bouillon boil 5 minutes with the dumplings. Some chopped parsley in the soup is very good.

No.13—STIRREDSPONGEDUMPLINGS.

Quantity for 6 Persons.

2 tbsps. of butter
6 tbsps. of flour
2 tbsps. of milk
¼ tsp. of salt
½ tsp. finely chopped parsley
1 pinch of nutmeg
2 eggs

Preparation: The butter is beaten to a cream, add yolks of 2 eggs, salt, parsley, nutmeg, flour and milk.

The whites of 2 eggs are beaten to a froth and stirred in. When the bouillon boils cut out small sponges with teaspoon and boil 5 minutes.

If the dumplings are too soft, add some more flour. The soup must be served at once.

No.14—CURDLESOUP .

Quantity for 6 Persons.

¾ pt. milk
2–3 eggs
3 tbsps. of flour
½ tsp. of salt
1 pinch of nutmeg
1 tsp. of finely chopped parsley

Preparation: The milk, eggs, flour, salt and nutmeg are well mixed.

When the bouillon boils the mass is slowly poured into it and boiled 5 minutes. The soup must be stirred constantly while boiling, lest it should burn. When served the parsley is added.

No.15—MARROWSTRIPSFORSOUP .

Quantity for 6 Persons.

⅛ lb. beef marrow, 2 rolls
⅛ lb. butter, (scant)
1 pinch of salt
1 pinch of white pepper

Preparation: The rolls are cut into equal strips and baked light brown in the butter. They are then placed on a platter. Soak the marrow in water, cut into layers and place on the hot bread. Sprinkle with salt and pepper and place the pan or platter into a hot oven. Leave it in the oven until the marrow is transparent and serve with the bouillon.

No.16—BREADSTICKSFORBOUILLON.

Quantity for 6 Persons.

½ pt. warm milk
½ cake yeast
1 tbsp. of milk
1 pinch of salt

Preparation: The warm milk and flour is beaten to a thin dough. The yeast is dissolved in a tablespoonful of warm milk and added to the dough. The whole is placed near a warm stove for rising which requires about ½ hour.

When this is done, work the dough with flour thick enough to roll out in ½ inch layer. Cut this dough into narrow strips 4 inches long and set aside for rising again, then bake them in a tin until, of a yellow color. Serve them fresh and warm with a strong bouillon.

No.17—CHEESESTICKSFORBOUILLON.

Quantity for 12 Persons.

⅛ lb. Swiss cheese
⅛ lb. Parmesan cheese
¼ lb. butter
¼ lb. flour
1 pinch salt
1 pinch paprika (red pepper)

Preparation: The butter is beaten to foam, the cheese is grated fine and added, also salt and paprika. Then the flour is kneaded into it to make a smooth dough and rolled out to ½ inch thickness. Cut in ½ inch strips and 5 inches long. Now bake in a medium hot oven to a light yellow color. If too dark the sticks will taste bitter.

They are served fresh and warm with strong bouillon.

No.18—CHEESEP ASTRY.

Quantity for 12—15 Persons.

¼ lb. flour
¼ lb. (scant) Parmesan cheese
⅛ lb. fresh, good butter
6 tbsps. thick, sour cream
1 pinch salt
1 pinch sugar
A little nutmeg
A little paprika (red pepper)

Preparation: The butter is beaten to a cream, and the finely grated cheese added. The cream, sugar, salt, nutmeg, paprika and flour added, made into a fine paste and rolled out into ½ inch thickness. Cut out with a small glass and bake in a medium hot oven to a light yellow color.

Remarks: It is better to put the paste on ice for a while and then roll it out. They are served hot with bouillon; or this pastry, as also the cheese sticks in No. 17 may be served as dessert instead of bread, butter and cheese.

No.19—FLOURDUMPLINGS.

Quantity for 6 Persons.

1 cup of flour
1½ cups of boiling water
1 tbsp. of butter

1 tsp. of salt, 1 egg

Preparation: The flour and salt are mixed and the boiling water, in which the butter is melted, poured on and the mass stirred briskly, after which the egg is mixed in.

The bouillon should be boiling, and the dumplings are formed or cut out with a teaspoon, put into the bouillon, and boiled 8 minutes.

Remarks: These dumplings may be made large, boiled in salt water 10 minutes and served with stewed fruit.

No.20—RICESOUPWITHBOUILLON.

Quantity for 6 Persons.

½ cup of rice
3 qts. of bouillon
2 cups of cold water

Preparation: The rice is washed and put on with 2 cups of cold water to boil 5 minutes; then pour off the water. Now add 3 qts. bouillon and cook slowly for 1 hour.

No.21—BOUILLONRICESOUPWITHT   OMATOES.

Quantity for 6 Persons.

½ cup rice
2 cups water
½ qt. canned tomatoes or 1½ lbs. fresh tomatoes.
3 qts. bouillon

Preparation: After the bouillon boils as in No. 1, add instead of one tomato the quantity mentioned in this recipe. Proceed as in No. 20, strain the bouillon and boil the rice in it for 1 hour.

No.22—RICE SOUP WITH MILK.

Quantity for 6 Persons.

1 cup of rice
3 cups of water
2 qts. of milk
½ tsp. of salt

Preparation: The rice is washed in water, and boiled for 5 minutes. Pour off the water and gradually add milk. It takes the rice about 1½ to 2 hours to get soft. Serve with sugar and cinnamon or cooked prunes.

In the summer time rice is palatable and refreshing, served cold with milk.

No.23—COLD RICE SOUP WITH APPLES.

Quantity for 6 Persons.

¾ cup of rice
2 qts. water
2 lbs. sweet-sour apples
½ lemon
¼ tsp. of salt
½ cup sugar

Preparation: The rice is washed and boiled in 2 cups of water for 5 minutes, then this water is poured off and 2 qts. added to boil 1 hour. In the meantime peel the apples and remove the core, cut them up in ⅛ths and put into rice, also cut up the ½ lemon in slices and add to the soup. Boil all this 20 minutes after adding salt and sugar as stated above.

If the soup is too thick, add some more water. It can be served warm, but it tastes better when cold.

Remarks: You can improve the soup by adding ½ pt. of white wine and more sugar.

No.24—BARLEYSOUPWITHBOUILLON.

Quantity for 6 Persons.

¾ cup of pearl barley
2 cups of water
3 qts. bouillon
Some finely cut asparagus

Preparations: The barley is washed in cold water and then brought to boiling in cold water. The water is poured off and the bouillon poured on and with this it is boiled slowly for 1½ hours. During the last ¾ of an hour the asparagus is put in and boiled until soft. If you wish, you may leave out the asparagus.

If the soup looks too white you may add some meat extract or stir into it the yolk of one egg.

No.25—BARLEYGRUELSOUPWITHBOUILLON.

Quantity for 6 Persons.

1 cup of pearl barley
1 tbsp. of butter
Some pieces of asparagus if you like
3 qts. strong bouillon

Preparation: The barley is washed and boiling water poured on and off twice. Heat the butter and cook the barley in it for a while. Then the bouillon is poured on and the soup is boiled slowly for 2½ hours. Now the soup is strained through a fine hair sieve and heated again.

If you wish some asparagus in it, which gives it a nice flavor, cook the asparagus pieces separately in bouillon until soft and add it to the soup, or stir the yolk of one egg into the soup.

This soup is very good for sick persons, but for this purpose the asparagus is left out.

No.26—BARLEYGRUELSOUP .

Quantity for 6 Persons.

1 cup of pearl barley
1 tbsp. of butter
3 qts. of water
Salt according to taste
1 pinch of nutmeg
2 tsps. of chopped parsley

Preparation: The barley is washed and put over the fire in some cold water. Let it get hot and pour off the water. Put the barley into the butter and let it steep a while, then add more water and boil for one hour. Add salt and nutmeg and at last add the parsley. You can also add a piece of fresh butter.

No.27—SWEETBARLEYGRUELSOUP .

Quantity for 6 Persons.

This soup is the same as <u>No. 26</u> with the exception of parsley and nutmeg which are left out. ½ cup of sugar and some cinnamon are added. The soup is then strained through a fine hair sieve and the yolk of one egg is stirred into it.

No.28—SAGOSOUPWITHBOUILLON.

Quantity for 6 Persons.

1 cup of sago
3 qts. of bouillon
1 qt. of water

Preparation: The sago is soaked for 1 hour in cold water. Pour off the water and add boiling hot bouillon, and in this the sago is left to boil until it is transparent.

No.29—SAGO SOUP WITH RED WINE OR RASPBERRY JUICE.

Quantity for 2 Persons.

¼ cup of sago
3 cups of water
½ cup of sugar
2 slices of lemon
1½ cups red wine or raspberry juice

Preparation: The sago is soaked in cold water for one hour. This water is then poured off and 3 cups of fresh water added in which the sago is boiled until soft and transparent. Add the quantity of red wine or juice, sugar and lemon and let it boil 5 minutes longer. Remove the lemon slices.

Serve this soup with zwieback or with small slices of toast.

No.30—FARINA SOUP WITH BOUILLON.

Quantity for 6 Persons.

¾ cup of farina
2 qts. of bouillon

Preparation: Let the already strained bouillon boil, then pour the farina into it slowly while stirring it, and leave it to boil 10 minutes.

No.31—GREEN CORN SOUP WITH BOUILLON.

Quantity for 6 Persons.

1½ cups of green corn
1 tbsp. of butter
3 qts. of bouillon
1 or 2 yolks of eggs

1 milk roll cut into small cubes
½ tbsp. of butter

Preparation: The green corn is steeped in the tablespoonful of butter, then the bouillon is added and this boiled slowly for 2 hours. This is then strained through a hair sieve and the yolk of one egg stirred in.

The milk roll is cut into cubes and fried in the ½ tablespoonful of butter until light yellow. When serving the soup put these bread cubes into it or serve them with the soup.

No.32—OA TMEALSOUP.

Quantity for 6 Persons.

2 cups of oatmeal
2 tbsps. of butter
Some salt
½ tsp. of meat extract
2½ qts. of water

Preparation: The oatmeal is put on with the water and salt and boiled slowly for ½ hour, then the soup is strained or pressed through a hair sieve. Now add butter and meat extract and let this all come to a boil. If the soup is too thick add some more boiling water.

Remarks: Instead of water you may also take milk and leave out the meat extract. You may add some sugar. Small pieces of rolls fried in butter are good with this soup. It is very good for invalids.

No.33—BEANSOUPWITHBOUILLON.

Quantity for 6 Persons.

1 cup of nice white beans
½ lb. of ham bones

3 qts. of good bouillon

Preparation: The beans are soaked in water for some hours, pour off the water, put on fresh water and bring to boil. After boiling for 10 minutes, pour off this water and boil again. Now pour it off for the last time, add the bouillon and boil the beans in this until soft. The ham bone is boiled in the bouillon. It requires 3 hours to cook this soup.

No.34—BEAN-PUREESOUPWITHCRABOR LOBSTERBUTTER.

Quantity for 4 Persons.

¾ cup of white beans
1½ qts. of water
1 tbsp. of butter
1 tbsp. of crab or lobster butter
1½ qts. of bouillon
Some white pepper
3 tbsps. of cream

Preparation: The beans are soaked, drained and boiled until soft in 1½ qts. of water. When they are soft the water must be all boiled down. Strain the beans through a fine sieve. This puree or mass is stewed in the butter and the crab or lobster butter and then the bouillon is added, also the white pepper. The cream is put into the soup dish and the soup is poured over it.

Begin preparation of this soup about 3 hours before time to serve.

No.35—PEASOUPWITHBOUILLON.

Quantity for 6 Persons.

1½ cups of peas
3 qts. of bouillon
½ tbsp. of butter

½ lb. ham or bones
1 roll

Preparation: The peas are prepared just like the beans in No. 33, then they are boiled until soft in bouillon for 3 hours. The soup is then strained. If it is ham that is being boiled in the bouillon, cut same into small pieces and put them into the strained peas.

Cut the roll into small cubes, fry them in butter until light yellow and serve with the soup.

No.36—LENTILSOUP .

Quantity for 6 Persons.

2 cups of lentils
3 qts. of bouillon
½ tbsp. of butter
1 tbsp. of flour
1 lb. of Wiener sausage

Preparation: The lentils are soaked in water for one hour, then this water is poured off and the lentils brought to boil in cold water. They must boil for 10 minutes. This water is again poured off and the bouillon added; in this the lentils are boiled until soft which requires 2½ to 3 hours. When the lentils are done, the butter is heated and the flour stirred into it; this is then poured into the soup. Ten minutes before serving put the Wieners into the soup, let come to a boil and then merely steep. The Wieners are served with the soup.

Remarks: Put very little salt into the soup, because the Wieners are already seasoned.

No.37—FRESHVEGET ABLESOUPWITHBOUILLON.

Quantity for 6 Persons.

3 small carrots
2 small kohlrabis
¼ head of celery
¼ head of cauliflower
30 pods of shelled peas
6 asparagus stalks
2 potatoes if you like
½ tbsp. of butter
1 tbsp. of flour
3 qts. bouillon

Preparation: The butter is heated and flour put into it to stew, then the bouillon is added; all vegetables and potatoes cut into smalls pieces, and put into the boiling bouillon and cooked for one hour until soft. If you cannot get all of these vegetables you may put less of it into the soup. Instead you may put small meat dumplings of veal or chicken into it. These dumplings are prepared as in recipe No. 10.

No.38—ASP ARAGUSSOUPWITHBOUILLON.

Quantity for 6 Persons.

2 lbs. of asparagus
3 qts. of bouillon
1 tbsp. of butter
2½ tbsps. of flour

Preparation: The butter is heated and the flour stewed in it, then the bouillon is added and let come to a boil. The asparagus is peeled, cut into small pieces, 1½ inches long, and boiled in the bouillon for ¾ of an hour.

If the asparagus is tender it will be done after ½ hour cooking.

No.39—CAULIFLOWERSOUPWITHBOUILLON.

Quantity for 6 Persons.

1 head of cauliflower
3 qts. bouillon
1 tbsp. of butter
2½ tbsps. of flour

Preparation: The preparation of this soup is the same as No. 38. The cauliflower is broken into small roses and boiled in the prepared bouillon about 20 minutes.

No.40—SORRELSOUPWITHBOUILLON.

Quantity for 6 Persons.

¼ lb. of sorrel
½ lb. lettuce leaves
¼ lb. butter
3 tbsps. of flour
2½ qts. bouillon
5 tbsps. of cream
Some sugar
1 pinch of pepper
1 roll cut into small cubes
½ tbsp. of butter
2 yolks of eggs

Preparation: The sorrel and lettuce leaves are put into boiling water for a minute and placed in a sieve to drain. It is then put into ¼ lb. of butter and stewed for 10 minutes. After this the mass is pressed through a sieve and stirred with the yolks of eggs and cream. The bouillon should be prepared and heated beforehand; the butter should be heated and the flour stirred in, and to this the bouillon is gradually added. The cubes of roll are fried light yellow in the ½ tablespoonful of butter. When the puree is done it is poured into the boiling bouillon and sugar and pepper put in to suit taste. The fried roll cubes are served with the soup.

No.41—CELERY SOUP WITH MILK.

Quantity for 6 Persons.

2 small bundles of fresh celery or 1½ head of celery
2 tbsps. of butter
3 tbsps. of flour
1½–2 qts. of milk and ½ qt. cream
1–2 yolks of eggs
1 pinch of pepper
1 pinch of salt

Preparation: The celery is cut into small pieces, and boiled in water until soft, then strained through a hair sieve. The butter is heated with the flour in it and the milk is now added. The boiled and strained celery is added, let come to a boil, stirring constantly. Add enough salt and pepper to suit your taste, stir in the yolks and serve at once. If you leave the soup standing it will get thick.

No.42—TOMATO SOUP.

Quantity for 6 Persons.

1 qt. canned tomatoes, or 4 lbs. of fresh tomatoes
1 qt. of water
1 tbsp. of butter
½ tsp. of sliced onions
1 pinch of pepper
Salt, some sugar
2 tbsps. of flour
1 roll cut into cubes
½ tbsp. of butter
1 tsp. of chopped parsley

Preparation: The tomatoes are boiled in water for a few minutes. If you have taken fresh tomatoes let them cook ½ hour in 1¼ qts. of water. Butter and finely cut onions are steeped so that the onions remain light yellow, add the flour and cook a little more. Butter, flour and onions are now put into the boiling tomatoes, and boiled with them. Then the mass is strained, sugar, salt, pepper added, the whole heated, the chopped parsley put in, and the soup served. The roll cubes are fried light yellow and put into the soup or if you wish you can serve them with the soup.

No.43—T OMATOSOUPWITHMILK.

Quantity for 6 Persons.

1 qt. canned tomatoes or 4 lbs. fresh tomatoes
1 qt. of milk
½ tbsp. of butter
1 pinch of salt
1 pinch of sugar
1 pinch of pepper
1 tsp. of baking soda

Preparation. The can of tomatoes is heated, the fresh tomatoes must be boiled until soft in ½ qt. of water, then pressed through a fine sieve.

The milk and butter are brought to boil in a double boiler and the tomatoes are put into it. Salt, pepper and sugar put in, then the soda stirred in and the soup served at once.

No.44—MOCK-TUR TLESOUP .

Quantity for 8 Persons.

½ calf's head without the brains
1 calf's tongue or 2 feet
⅛ lb. of raw ham, (scant)
1 carrot
1 piece of parsley root
½ of a celery root
2 small onions

⅛ qt. red wine
Salt and pepper
⅛ lb. of butter
⅛ lb. of flour
1/16 qt. of Madeira wine
4 eggs
2½ qts. of water

Preparation: The finely cut ham, soup greens and onions are fried and the calf's head and tongue or chopped feet are then put in and the quantity of water added. The feet must be scalded before using.

The whole is cooked until tender and salt and pepper added. Then it is strained. The skin of the calf's head is cut into small pieces (also the tongue and feet) a little salt is strewn over the meat and the red wine poured over it.

Butter and flour are browned and the bouillon, from which the fat has been removed is poured on, also the Madeira wine.

The soup is now slowly boiled for one hour. The scum and fat must be taken off.

Now the meat with the red wine are put in.

The eggs are boiled hard and the whole yolks put into the soup. You can also cut the yolks in halves and put one-half into each soup dish.

It requires 3 hours to cook this soup.

No.45—POT ATOSOUPWITHBOUILLON.

Quantity for 6 Persons.

2 lbs. of raw or unboiled peeled potatoes
2 qts. bouillon of ox bones (soup-bones) or bouillon of rabbitroast bones, or bouillon of poultryroast bones
1 roll cut into small cubes
½ tbsp. of butter

Preparation: The potatoes are pared, cut into small pieces and cooked until soft in the bouillon, then pressed through a sieve. If you wish you may leave the pieces of potatoes whole.

The roll cubes are toasted light yellow and put into the soup or served with it.

Remarks: Potato soup of rabbitroast bones or fowl bones is very good. If there is some meat left on these bones, cut it in small pieces and put it into the soup.

No.46—POT ATOSOUP .

Quantity for 6 Persons.

2 lbs. of raw potatoes
2 qts. of water
1½ tbsps. of fresh butter
Salt
1 roll cut into cubes
½ tbsp. of butter
½ tsp. of meat extract

Preparation: The potatoes are pared, cut into small pieces, and cooked until soft in the 2 qts. of water, then pressed through a sieve and cooked again. Salt, butter, meat extract are now added.

The roll cubes are fried light yellow in the ½ tablespoonful of butter and put into the soup before serving.

No.47—WHITEWINESOUP .

Quantity for 6 Persons.

1 qt. light white wine
1 qt. water
1 stick of cinnamon

2 cloves
2 tsps. of lemon sugar or 4 slices of lemon
¼ lb. of sugar
3 tbsps. of corn starch or flour
1 pinch of salt
3 eggs

Preparation: The water with the spices is boiled for 2 minutes before the wine is added and let come to a boil again. The yolks of the 3 eggs are stirred with flour and a little water and then stirred into the soup. Let it come to a boil once more, stirring constantly. Then it is taken from the stove. The whites of the eggs are beaten to a stiff froth and put into the soup when served.

Cloves, lemon slices, and cinnamon are taken out. Zwieback or toasted slices of rolls are served with this soup.

No.48—REDWINESOUP .

Quantity for 6 Persons.

1 qt. light red wine
1 qt. of water
1 small piece of lemon peel
3 cloves
1 stick of cinnamon
¼ lb. of sugar
3 tbsps. of cornstarch or common flour

Preparation: Boil the water, sugar and spices for 10 minutes. The flour mixed with some water is stirred in and let come to a boil, stirring constantly.

Heat the red wine and put it into the soup but do not boil any longer. Serve at once. Serve zwieback or small soup macaroons with it.

No.49—BEERSOUP .

Quantity for 6 Persons.

1½ qts. of beer
½ qt. water
1 stick of cinnamon
2 cloves
1 pinch of salt
3 tbsps. of flour or cornstarch
3 slices of lemon or lemon sugar
3 eggs
¼ lb. sugar

Preparation: Water, beer, sugar and spices are brought to a boil. The flour and yolks of eggs are mixed with water and stirred into the soup and brought to a boil again. The whites of eggs are beaten to a stiff froth and put into the soup when served.

Zwieback or toasted slices of rolls are served with the soup.

No.50—APPLESOUP .

Quantity for 6 Persons.

2 lbs. of apples
2 qts. of water
¼ lb. of sugar
1 stick of cinnamon
2 tbsps. of cornstarch
⅛ lb. of currants
Juice of ½ lemon and a small piece of rind

Preparation: The apples with their peelings on are cut into pieces and the core removed, and then boiled in the water with the spices until soft. The flour is mixed with a little water and put into the apples while boiling.

Then the whole is strained or pressed through a sieve. Now the washed currants are added and a cup of red wine or white wine and cooked again.

Remarks: All fruit soups may be prepared this way, i.e., plum, cherry, apricots, strawberries, raspberries, currants, grapes, gooseberries or rhubarb soups are made this way but some need more sugar than others, or the wine is left out.

Dried fruit may also be used.

No.51—R YE BREAD SOUP .

Quantity for 6 Persons.

2 lbs. of rye bread
2 qts. of water
Salt
1 tumbler full of white wine
Some sugar, about 1 tbsp.
1 tbsp. of fresh butter
½ cup of currants

Preparation: The rye bread which may be stale is put on with 2 qts. of cold water and boiled a little, then pressed through a hair sieve.

If it should be too thick, leave out some bread. It is then boiled with the salt, sugar, currants and butter for a little while. The white wine is poured into the soup dish and the soup added to it while boiling hot.

No.52—FLOUR SOUP ,(WHEA T).

Quantity for 6 Persons.

⅛ lb. of butter
⅛ lb. of flour
½ qt. of water
1 pinch of salt

1½ qts. of milk

Preparation: The butter is browned, flour stirred in, milk, water and salt added. The soup must be boiled 20 minutes, constantly stirring it. You may stir into it the yolk of one egg.

No.53—R YEFLOURSOUP .

Quantity for 6 Persons.

⅛ lb. of rye flour
2 tbsps. of butter
½ qt. of water
1 qt. of milk
1 pinch of salt
2 yolks of eggs

Preparation: The rye flour is stirred into the cold water, butter and salt added and cooked for 20 minutes while stirring constantly. Add the milk and boil again; then stir in the yolks.

No.54—MILKSOUP .

Quantity for 6 Persons.

2 qts. of milk
1 small stick of cinnamon
1 tbsp. of lemon sugar
⅛ lb. of sugar
1 pinch of salt
⅛ lb. cornstarch

Preparation: 1½ qts. milk, sugar, spices and salt, let come to a boil. The flour is mixed with ½ qt. of milk and stirred into the boiling milk, then boiled for ¼ hour. Stir in one egg yolk, then serve.

No.55—CHOCOLATESOUP.

Quantity for 6 Persons.

2 qts. of milk
½ lb. of sweet chocolate or ⅛ lb. of cocoa
1 tbsp. of lemon sugar
¼ lb. of sugar
1 small stick of cinnamon
1 pinch of salt
⅛ lb. of cornstarch

Preparation: Prepare the chocolate soup just the same as the milk soup No. 54. Grate the chocolate and stir it into the flour or cornstarch and milk. If it gets too thick add more milk.

No. 56—FISH SOUP WITH FISH DUMPLINGS.

Quantity for 6 Persons.

2½ lbs. of pickerel or other fish
1½ qts. of water
½ of an onion, salt
⅛ lb. of flour
⅛ lb. of butter
1 qt. of bouillon
8 oysters
15 shrimps or crabs
⅛ qt. white wine
2 tbsps. of butter
2 yolks of eggs
12 small fish dumplings

Preparation: The fish is scaled, drawn and washed. The meat is cut from the bones, the liver and gall removed. The bones are chopped up and with water, onions, salt and spices slowly stewed for a fish bouillon.

Melt ⅛ lb. butter, stir in the flour, simmer to a light yellow, pour the fish bouillon in, let it simmer slowly for ¾ of an hour.

The crawfish or crabs are boiled in the meantime. The meat is taken out of the shells. The oysters and the fish liver, which is cut into pieces, are heated in the white wine, but not boiled. The meat of the pickerel is also cut into small pieces and stewed in 2 tablespoonfuls of butter until tender.

The fish dumplings are also cooked 10 minutes in the white wine. When done, put the dumplings into the soup tureen. All the meat, liver, crabs and oysters are put into the soup tureen, the gravy is strained and the yolks of 2 eggs stirred in and then poured into the tureen. Salt to taste. It is a very fine soup.

The fish dumplings are made the same way as the meat dumplings in No. 10, only instead of meat take fish, and take half the quantities given in

<u>No. 10</u>. Leave out the nutmeg.

No. 57—CRAWFISH OR CRAB SOUP WITH MARROW DUMPLINGS OR LIVER DUMPLINGS.

Quantity for 6–8 Persons.

24 small crabs
¼ lb. of butter
2½ qts. of bouillon
1 pinch of white pepper

Preparation: The crabs are washed carefully and thrown into boiling salt water, but taken out again immediately. Mash the crab meat and stew it ¼ of an hour in the ¼ lb. of butter. After this stir in the bouillon, cover and cook slowly 1 hour.

Marrow dumplings or liver dumplings are cooked in the soup which has been strained. The marrow dumplings are prepared as directed in <u>No. 7</u> and the liver dumplings as in <u>No. 9</u>. Take the same quantities. Serve at once when the dumplings are done.

No. 58—OYSTER SOUP.

Quantity for 6 Persons.

1 qt. oysters
1 qt. milk
1 pinch of salt
1 pinch of pepper
2 tbsps. of fresh butter

Preparation: The milk is boiled and butter, salt, and pepper added. The oysters with their juice are put into the boiling milk; stir constantly while doing this, let come to boiling, stirring continually; then serve at once. Serve crackers with the soup.

No. 59—CHICKEN BOUILLON TO DRINK.

Quantity for 4 Persons.

1 chicken
1 egg
1½ qts. of water
Some salt

Preparation: The chicken is cleaned well and all fat removed. The meat is removed from the bones and chopped fine, the bones cracked or split, the egg is stirred in and with water and salt put into a covered pot and cooked slowly for 3 hours. Strain through a sieve and serve. This soup is very good for invalids and convalescents.

No. 60—PIGEON BOUILLON TO DRINK.

Quantity for 3 Persons.

2 pigeons
1 egg
1¼ qts. of water
Some salt

Preparation: The pigeons are cleaned well and washed. The meat is removed from the bones and chopped fine, the bones split or cracked and the egg stirred in. Put on the fire with the water and salt and cook in a covered pot for 3 hours. Strain and serve. This soup is also good for sick people.

No. 61—PIGEON SOUP.

Quantity for 6–8 Persons.

2 old pigeons
2 lbs. of soup bone, or better

1 lb. of beef
Some soup greens
3 qts. of water
Scarcely ¼ lb. of fine barley
2 tbsps. of butter
2 yolks of eggs
4 asparagus stalks

Preparation: The pigeons are cleaned well and the breast and clubs or legs cut off and left whole. The other meat is chopped, also the beef, and all is boiled until soft in the quantity of water with salt and soup greens. In the meantime the barley is soaked. Drain well and stew the barley in butter for a little while, then gradually pour on the strained bouillon.

Peel the asparagus and cut it into inch lengths and add to the barley and bouillon. Boil for 1 hour. The meat from the breast and legs is cut fine and put into the soup when served. If you have used beef for the soup you may make hash or salad of it.

No. 62—CHICKEN SOUP.

Quantity for 6 Persons.

1 chicken
2½ qts. of water
Some soup greens
Salt
6 asparagus stalks, a few pieces of cauliflower
¼ cup of good rice, good measure
¼ tsp. of meat extract

Preparation: The chicken is cleaned well, washed and cooked until soft with soup greens, salt and water which requires 1½ hours. If it is an old chicken it will require 2 to 3 hours. The rice is washed and put on with some cold water to get partly done. When the water is all boiled down add the strained bouillon.

The asparagus and cauliflower are cleaned and cut into small pieces and cooked until soft with the rice in the bouillon. When the soup is done the meat extract is added.

The chicken breast is cut into small pieces and put into the soup. You can also carve the whole chicken and serve it with the soup.

No. 63—PARTRIDGE SOUP.

Quantity for 6 Persons.

2 old partridges
4 potatoes cut in cubes
2 carrots cut in pieces
3 tbsps. of flour
2 tbsps. of butter
Salt
2 qts. of water
1½ tbsps. of butter

Preparation: The partridges are cleaned well and fried in the 2 tablespoonfuls of butter to a light brown. The flour is browned in the 1½ tablespoonfuls of butter and the water added, also potatoes, carrots and salt and the fried partridges; all of this is boiled until tender in a covered pot. This will require 2 to 2½ hours. The partridge breast is cut in pieces and served in the soup.

The remaining partridge meat may be utilized in hash or dumplings.

No. 64—WILD GAME OR POULTRY SOUP.

Quantity for 4–6 Persons.

You can make soups from all kinds of wild or tame birds. Follow directions given for chicken, pigeon or partridge soup. If the soup is made of bones and remnants and not rich enough you may add meat extract.

No. 65—RED WINE SOUP WITH SAGO.

Quantity for 6 Persons.

¾ bottle of red wine
1 qt. of water
¼ lb. of sago
1 stick of cinnamon
¼ lb. of sugar
2 slices of lemon
½ cup raisins

Preparation: The sago and raisins are boiled until soft in the water. Then the red wine is added, also cinnamon, sugar and lemon slices, and the soup is brought to boil again. Zwieback or toasted rolls are served with it.

No. 66—TOMATO SOUP WITH SMALL MEAT OR POTATO DUMPLINGS.

Quantity for 6 Persons.

1 qt. can of tomatoes
1 qt of water
1½ tbsps. of butter
2 heaping tbsps. of flour
¼ tbsp. of sliced onions
Salt to suit taste
1 pinch of pepper
1 tbsp. of sugar

Meat Dumplings.

¼ lb. beef
¼ lb. pork
1 egg
Salt and pepper to suit taste
1 tbsp. of butter

Potato Dumplings.

½ cup grated potatoes
½ egg
2 tbsps. of flour
Salt and pepper to suit taste

Preparation: Tomatoes are cooked in the water for 10 minutes. The butter is melted and the onions put in and stewed a little, then the flour is stirred in and the whole is put into the soup. Salt, pepper and sugar are added and after a few minutes boiling the whole is strained.

The meat dumplings contain beef, pork, 1 egg, butter, salt and pepper, which is all mixed and small dumplings are formed.

The potato dumplings are made of mashed or grated boiled potatoes which are mixed with 1 egg, flour, salt and pepper. Small dumplings are formed and rolled in flour.

The tomato soup must be boiling when the dumplings are put in, and boil 10 minutes. Serve the soup at once with the dumplings in it.

A teaspoonful of finely chopped parsley may be put in the soup.

No. 67—BUTTERMILK SOUP OR SOUR MILK SOUP.

Quantity for 6 Persons.

1½ qts. of buttermilk or sour milk
½ qt. sweet milk
¼ lb. of sago
1 small stick of cinnamon
3 slices of lemon
1 pinch of salt
1 cup of sugar

Preparation: Buttermilk and sweet milk are brought to a boil with the sago. Cinnamon and lemon added. Cook slowly for one hour, stirring frequently. Add salt and a little sugar. The soup may be served hot or cold.

No. 68—OYSTER PLANT SOUP.

Quantity for 6 Persons.

2 bundles of oyster plants
2½ tbsps. of butter
2 tbsps. of flour
1 pinch of pepper
Salt to suit your taste
2 yolks of eggs
1½ qts. of milk

Preparation: The oyster plants are scraped and cut into small pieces. Put the clean oyster plants immediately into water mixed with vinegar and flour so that they will not get black.

When they are well cleaned they are stewed with the butter and a little water until tender; then stir in the flour and cook a few minutes. Then the milk is gradually added while stirring the soup constantly. Now the soup is left to cook a little, stirring occasionally and then salt and pepper are added.

At last the yolks of 2 eggs are stirred in.

CHAPTER 2.
BEEF.

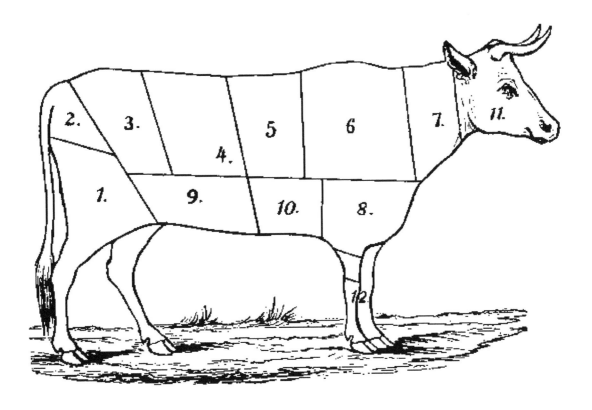

1. Beef Round
2. Rump
3. Sirloin
4. Loin and Porterhouse with Fillet
5–6. Rib Roast
6. Chuck of Beef
7. Neck
8. Round Shoulder
9. Beef Flank
10. Beef Brisket
11. Head
12. Shank
13. Tail

Preparation of All Kinds of Beef Dishes. Boiled, Roasted and Salted Beef. How Remnants of Beef May be Utilized.

The best quality of beef has a nice red color and white suet. The meat of young cows is more pale and tender.

Old cows have dark, brownish red meat and yellow suet.

Young beef makes a good roast, but a poor bouillon.

Old beef makes a tough roast, but a good bouillon.

The best Pieces for Roasting.

The fillet, roast beef, and the inner part of the forerib.

The best Pieces for braising or Pot Roast.

The rump, the sirloin, the fillet, roast beef, (well hung), also the chuck and round shoulder, (well hung).

The best Pieces for Bouillon.

The meat from the round, the rump, the chuck, in fact all lean meat and bones.

Meat for Salting and Pickling.

The meat from the round, also from the brisket, but without bones.

Best Pieces for Boiling.

The rump, the brisket and chuck.

No. 1—ROAST BEEF.

Quantity for 6–8 Persons.

6 lbs. of roast beef
2–3 tbsps. of butter
½ of an onion, to suit taste
½ cup of water
1 cup of water for gravy
¾ tbsp. of flour

Salt, pepper

Preparation: The roast beef is salted and peppered, put into a roasting pan with the quantity of water given and roasted in the oven. After ½ hour's roasting add 2 to 3 tablespoonfuls of butter and let it roast for another hour, basting frequently. In 1½ hours the roast beef is rare inside and in 2 hours it is well done.

If the roast is small, it will require 15 minutes less per pound, and if larger 15 minutes longer for roasting. When the roast is done, put it on a platter and make the gravy.

Take ¾ tablespoonful of flour, put it into the pan, stir it well and let it boil 3 minutes, then pour in the 1 cup of water, boil a few minutes, strain and serve.

Remarks: Be careful that the butter does not turn too dark during the roasting. Should this be the case add a little water, so that the gravy may not taste bitter.

No. 2—MEAT PUDDING.

How to Utilize Roast Beef.

Roast Beef With Rice Covering.

Quantity for 4–6 Persons.

1¼ lbs. left over roast beef
½ cup of rice
2 tbsps. of grated Swiss or Parmesan cheese
½ tbsp. of flour
¼ tsp. chopped onions
2 tbsps. of butter
2 tbsps. of grated rolls
½ cup of left over gravy
½ qt. of bouillon or water
2 yolks of eggs

Preparation: The roast meat is chopped, but not too fine, and stewed in a pan with the butter and onions. The gravy is mixed with flour, salt and pepper and poured on the meat which is left to cook a few minutes until the gravy gets thick.

The rice is cooked until soft and thick in the water or bouillon, the grated cheese is put in and at last the yolks of 2 eggs. Taste the rice for salt. Butter a pudding mold and strew in some grated rolls, now put in one layer of rice and one layer of meat and so on until all the meat and rice are in. Close the mold well and set in a steamer over a kettle of boiling water and steam for 2 hours.

After the pudding is done, turn it out and pour over it a Dutch gravy or serve the gravy separately with it.

No. 3—BEEF FILLET ROAST.

Quantity for 6–8 Persons.

4–6 lbs. of fillet
¼ lb. of butter
Salt and pepper
½ cup sweet or sour cream
½ cup of water
For larding take ⅛ lb. of bacon
½ tbsp. of flour

Preparation: The fillet roast is freed from fat and skin. The bacon is cut in narrow strips and the fillet larded with it.

The butter is put into the frying pan and heated and then the fillet browned in it on both sides and sprinkled with salt and pepper. It is roasted in the oven for ¾ of an hour, basting frequently with the gravy or water; the cream is put on 1 spoonful at a time. The roast must be of a nice pink color. It is placed on a platter.

The gravy: The given quantity of flour is put into the pan and browned, the water poured over and cooked for a few minutes; then strain and serve.

You can also put champignons into the gravy, which makes it richer.

No. 4—BEEF FILLET BEEFSTEAK.

Quantity for 6 Persons.

2½ lbs. of fillet
¼ lb. of butter
Salt and pepper
¼ cup of water

Preparation: Cut the 2½ lbs. of fillet into 6 pieces, trim off the fat and skin and pound slightly. They are then formed into round beefsteaks and sprinkled with salt and pepper.

The butter is put into a frying pan and heated and the steaks quickly browned on both sides, which requires about 5 minutes. Fry for 5 minutes more, basting and turning occasionally. The steaks are then taken out and put on a platter. The water poured into the butter and boiled a little while; this gravy is put over the steak. Beefsteak is fried in an open frying pan on the top of the stove.

No. 5—BEEF FILLET STEAKS WITH CHAMPIGNONS AND FRIED GOOSE LIVER.

Quantity for 6 Persons.

2½ lbs. of fillet
¼ lb. of butter
Salt and pepper
¼ cup of water
½ lb. goose liver
½ lb. champignons
½ tbsp. of butter
¼ tsp. of flour

2 tbsps. of sweet cream
⅛ tsp. of meat extract
⅛ lb. of butter with it

Preparation: The fillet is prepared just the same as in <u>No. 4</u>, and also fried the same way. The goose liver is salted and peppered and sprinkled with flour, then fried light yellow in ⅛ lb. of butter; add 1 tablespoonful of water, cover the pan and stew ¼ hour longer.

The water having been drained off the champignons, add ½ tablespoonful of butter, ¼ teaspoonful of flour and a little salt and then cook a little. The cream and meat extract are added and simmered a while longer.

The ready fried beefsteaks are put on a hot platter. The goose liver is cut into as many pieces as there are steaks, and one piece put in the center of each steak. The prepared champignons are placed around each piece of goose liver on top of each steak.

The gravy is put on the platter too. You can garnish the platter with scallops of puff paste. This dish is nice between courses.

No. 6—BROILED STEAK OF ROAST BEEF.

Quantity for 6 Persons.

3 lbs. of roast beef
Salt, pepper
¼ lb. of butter (scant)

Preparation: The roast beef is cut into 1½ inch thick slices and pounded well. A broiler is put on the open medium hot fire and the slices laid on to broil for 20 minutes, turning frequently. Put them on a hot platter, sprinkle with pepper and salt, cut the butter into small pieces and place them on the hot meat. Serve at once.

No. 7—STEAK FROM THE BEEF ROUND.

Quantity for 6 Persons.

3–4 lbs. round steak
¼ lb. of butter
Salt, pepper
¼ cup of water
1 onion

Preparation: The meat is cut into slices ¾ inch thick and pounded slightly.

The butter is heated; the onion is sliced and fried till light yellow in the butter, then taken out and the meat put into this hot onion butter after it has been salted and peppered. Fry for 5 to 8 minutes to a light brown, turning it once or twice.

The meat is put on a hot platter and the onions on top. A little water is put into the pan with butter and boiled a little. This gravy is poured over the meat. Serve at once.

Remarks: If you do not like onions, omit them.

No. 8—CHOPPED GERMAN STEAK OR HAMBURG STEAK.

Quantity for 6 Persons.

2½ lbs. chopped steak
1 tbsp. of butter
2–3 eggs
Salt, pepper
1 tsp. of grated onion
⅙ lb. of butter

Preparation: The lean meat from the round is chopped fine or ground fine by putting it twice or three times through the grinder, then salted, peppered and mixed with the eggs, a tablespoonful of butter and onion if you like. If you do not like onions, omit them.

After mixing well, scant ¼ lb. dumplings are formed and flattened to 1½ inches in thickness. The butter or lard heated, the steaks put in and fried about 10 minutes, turning and basting frequently.

Serve the steaks on a hot platter, and for gravy pour a little water into the frying pan with the butter, let come to a boil, and pour over the steaks.

Remarks: You may serve mustard gravy with this steak by adding 2 teaspoonfuls of mustard to the steak butter and 1 teaspoonful of flour and bouillon or water, boiled for 2 minutes and strained.

No. 9 RAW BEEFSTEAK A LA TARTARE.

Quantity for 6 Persons.

2 lbs. of chopped meat
Salt, some pepper
6 yolks of eggs
2 tsps. of chopped onions
2 pepper-pickles
2 salt pickles
⅛ lb. sardines
1½ tbsps. of capers

Preparation: The beef which must be very fresh and free from sinews, is chopped or ground twice in the grinder. Mix with salt and pepper and form into 6 equal 1¼ inch thick steaks. With a knife, score or mark squares on the surface. Make a depression in the middle of each steak and put into this carefully one raw yolk of egg. Garnish each steak with a small heap of onions, chopped small pieces of pickles, sardines from which the bones have been removed. Capers and mustard mixed with oil and vinegar may be served with it. The steaks must be served fresh.

No. 10—FILLET BEEFSTEAK FOR BREAKFAST.

Quantity for 2 Persons.

1 lb. of fillet meat
⅛ lb. of butter
½ onion
Some salt
1 pinch of pepper
6 tbsps. of gravy
4 potatoes peeled

Preparation: The pan which must have a cover is buttered. The potatoes and onions are cut into cubes, salted and peppered and put into the pan.

The pounded meat, cut into slices is browned on both sides in 1 tablespoonful of butter from the ⅛ lb. This must be done quickly in about one minute. The browned meat is then put on the raw potatoes. The gravy is poured into the beefsteak butter, or if you have no gravy, take water and boil it for one minute with a little meat extract, pour it over the potatoes and meat, cover well, and cook it 5 minutes over a hot fire; then set it aside and cook it slowly for 20 minutes more. Serve it at once in the covered pan. The pan must be small for such a small portion.

Remarks: Instead of potatoes and onions you can take fresh or canned champignons, morels or mushrooms. This dish is good for sick persons if you omit the onions and mushrooms and take potatoes only.

No. 11—BEEF POT ROAST.

Quantity for 6 Persons.

4 lbs. of meat
1 piece of fat bacon
Salt
6 pepper-corns
1 bay-leaf
1 clove
2 tbsps. of suet
3 tbsps. of flour

1 tbsp. of red wine or Madeira
½ of an onion

Preparation: The meat—from rump, chuck or sirloin—is pounded. The bacon cut in small thick pieces is stuck into the meat, heat the suet, add onions and brown meat slightly on both sides. When this is done it is placed on a platter. Flour is browned in the suet to which water and the spices are added, and cooked. The browned meat is put into the gravy, which should cover it. Cover the pot well. The best thing for a pot roast is an iron pot. Put the covered roast into the moderately hot oven for 2½ to 3 hours, basting frequently. One-half hour before done, pour the wine over it. When done, take the roast out and prepare the gravy. Take off all fat; if too thick add more water and strain.

No. 12—BRAISED BEEF SLICES.

Quantity for 6 Persons.

3 slices of meat, 3 lbs.
Salt, pepper
⅛ lb. of butter
½ qt. of bouillon
10 small peeled onions
3 carrots cut into cubes
1½ tbsps. of flour
1½ tbsps. of vinegar

Preparation: The meat slices are salted, pounded, browned in hot butter and put into a pot. The carrots and onions are added and the bouillon is poured over. Cook slowly until tender.

The meat, carrots and onions are taken out with a big skimmer. The flour is browned in the butter in which the meat was first browned, the gravy of the meat added and the vinegar; boil and strain. The onions and carrots are arranged around the roast slices and a few tablespoonfuls of the gravy put on the meat. You can also add for garnishing some nice cuts of boiled potatoes or small potato dumplings.

No. 13—ROASTED RIB PIECE.

Quantity for 6 Persons.

4 lbs.—2 ribs
Some fine spices, salt
¾ qts. good vinegar
⅛ lb. of butter
2 kohlrabis cut in cubes
¼ celery root cut in cubes
½ parsley root cut in cubes
2 onions, cut up small
3 carrots cut in cubes

Preparation: The bones and tendons are taken out, the meat is then rubbed with salt and the spices and put into vinegar for ½ hour. The vegetables, which have been cut into small pieces, are stewed in the given quantity of butter until soft. Add salt, and a little water from time to time to prevent the vegetables from becoming brown. The meat is fried in a pan with butter or lard for ½ hour, turning occasionally. One-half of this fried meat is put into a flat pan, the stewed vegetables are put on top and the other half of the meat is placed on top of this and the whole is thus baked ¾ hour in a medium hot oven. From time to time drop on a little butter.

When serving, be careful to place the roast on the platter without dropping some of the vegetables. The gravy may be served with it.

Remarks: When the roast is ready for baking you can roll it in a piece of oiled paper and bake it in that.

No. 14—SOUR ROAST.

Quantity for 6 Persons.

4 lbs. of meat
2 qts. of vinegar
1 onion cut in slices
10 pepper-corns

3 bay-leaves
3 cloves
Some salt
2½ tbsps. of flour
2 tbsps. of drippings
½ glass red wine
⅛ lb. of bacon

Preparation: For the sour roast take the same kind of meat as in No. 11, pound it, put it into vinegar with the spices and leave it in that for 4 days, turning it over once in a while. After this time take it out and lard it with bacon cut into pieces one-third inch thick and 2½ inches long. Pierce the meat with a pointed knife and insert the bacon.

Heat the lard and fry the meat light brown on both sides and place it on a platter. Brown the flour in the lard and pour on the vinegar with the spices, water and salt. Put in a piece of honey cake (Pfeffer Kuchen) if on hand, and ½ tablespoonful of sugar, boil all and put the roasted meat into this gravy. Cover the roast and bake in the oven for 2½ to 3 hours, turning and basting frequently with the gravy. One-half hour before done, pour in the red wine.

When the roast is tender, finish the gravy. Put the roast on a platter, take all grease off the gravy and strain it. If it is too thick, add more water, if not sour enough, add more vinegar.

Potato dumplings or noodles are good with this roast.

No. 15—BEEF ROULADE.

Quantity for 6 Persons.

2–2½ lbs. of beef cut into ½ inch thick slices
¼ lb. bacon cut into thin slices
1 onion chopped fine
Salt, pepper
1½ tbsps. of flour
⅛ lb. of butter or lard

1½ cups of bouillon or water

Preparation: The best meat for this is from the round. The meat slices are pounded and cut into squares, then sprinkled with salt and pepper, covered with bacon and onions, rolled up and fastened with twine or toothpicks.

Heat the butter or lard and brown the roulades in it, sprinkle flour over and stew, adding some salt and the bouillon or water. Then stew slowly for 1 hour in a covered pan or pot. If the roulades are small it requires less time, if large it requires from 2 to 2½ hours. The roulades are served with the gravy after the twine or toothpicks have been removed.

No. 16—BEEF GULASH.

Quantity for 6 Persons.

2 lbs. of meat
2 small onions in cubes
1 tbsp. of lard
Salt
1 pinch of paprika
1 cup of water
1 tbsp. of flour

Preparation: The onions are stewed in the lard. The meat is cut into pieces 1½ inches thick and 1½ inches square and added to the stewed onions, stewed 10 minutes, flour, salt and pepper added, and stewed 10 minutes longer, and then 1 cup of water poured over. In a covered pot or pan it is now stewed for 2 to 2½ hours, stirring often. If it gets too dry, pour on more water. Gulash must not be too juicy. A little red wine may be added.

Remarks: From leavings of roast beef fillets or pot roast you can prepare gulash in ½ hour. Instead of water you may use the left over gravy.

No. 17—STEAMED BEEF-BRISKET.

Quantity for 6–8 Persons.

6 lbs. of beef brisket
Salt
Soup greens
1 small onion
8 pepper-corns
2 cloves
2 yolks of eggs
1½ tbsps. of Parmesan cheese, grated
2 tbsps. grated rolls
1½ tbsps. of butter
6 qts. water
1 bay-leaf

Preparation: The beef is pounded and tied into a white cloth in a good shape. The water is heated with salt, soup greens and spices to the boiling point, then the meat added which must boil 1 hour so little that you hardly notice it. The pot must be well covered. If there are bones in the meat, they should be removed and put into the stock.

When the meat is tender, take it out, cover it with fricassee gravy which is first stirred with 2 yolks of eggs. Strew the Parmesan cheese and roll crumbs over it and baste with some melted butter. Now set it into the oven and bake for 20 minutes. You can garnish the roast with fried cut potatoes or macaroni.

Cucumber salad, mixed pickles or salt- or pepper-pickles go nicely with this meat.

Remarks: The bouillon may be boiled down and used for soup.

No. 18—BEEF CUTLETS OF ROAST BEEF.

Quantity for 6 Persons.

3 lbs. roast beef
Salt, pepper
¼ lb. butter

Preparation: The meat is cut into 3 slices and bones, tendons, fat and skin removed from it. It is then pounded well. It must be 1½ inches thick. The butter is heated, the meat fried 20 minutes, turning it over several times. The last 5 minutes you put it off the hot fire and let it simmer. Sprinkle with salt and pepper, then baste with the butter. Serve on a hot platter and garnish with parsley. The remnants may be used for gulash.

No. 19—BOILED BEEF.

Quantity for 6 Persons.

4 lbs. of meat
Soup greens
1 lb. of bones
4–5 qts. of water
Salt

Preparation: The meat which may be from the rump, thick rib piece or breast, is washed. The water with the bones, all soup greens and salt is boiled for 1 hour, then put in the meat and boil slowly 2½ hours. With this meat serve onion, mustard, horse radish or leek gravy.

Remarks: This meat may be utilized for hash, salad, meat pudding or beef with onions and eggs.

No. 20—BEEF HASH.

1 lb. remnants of meat
¼ of an onion
1 tbsp. of butter
½ wine glass of white wine

1 cup bouillon
Salt, pepper
1 tsp. of flour

Preparation: The meat is chopped fine and may be of soup meat, roast or steak. The onions are cut fine and stewed in butter, then the chopped meat put in, the flour strewn over it, simmered a little while longer, salt and pepper added and bouillon. If you take water add ¼ tablespoonful of meat extract and wine. Let it cook ¼ hour and serve. Fresh boiled, peeled potatoes are nice to serve with it.

No. 21—HASH WITH POTATOES.

Quantity for 4–6 Persons.

1—1½ lbs. of meat (boiled or roasted beef)
¼ onion
1 tbsp. of butter
A little pepper
Salt
1 cup of bouillon or water
4 peeled, boiled potatoes

Preparation: The meat is chopped fine. The onions are cut fine and steeped in the butter, then the meat put in and cooked 5 minutes. Salt and pepper are added, the potatoes are also chopped fine and added and water or bouillon poured on. The whole is cooked for ¼ of an hour, then served.

No. 22—BEEF WITH ONIONS.

Quantity for 6 Persons.

1½ lbs. boiled beef
1 onion
2 tbsps. of butter or suet

2 tbsps. of flour
1 tbsp. of vinegar
1 pinch of pepper
Salt
½ tsp. of meat extract
½ qt. of bouillon

Preparation: The onion is cut fine and simmered in the butter or suet until soft; then add flour, simmer until brown; pour on the bouillon, vinegar, salt, pepper and meat extract and let come to a boil.

The meat is cut in slices and put into the gravy and heated.

No. 23—BOILED BEEF SLICES FRIED WITH EGGS AND ONIONS.

Quantity for 6 Persons.

1½ lbs. boiled beef
1 onion
2 tbsps. of butter or good drippings
6 eggs
Salt
1 pinch of pepper

Preparation: Meat and onions are cut into inch thick slices. Sprinkle with salt and pepper and fry in the butter or lard until light brown. Put the meat and onions on a hot platter. Fry the eggs in butter, strew salt over and lay them on each slice of meat. Be careful to keep the yolk whole.

Potato salad is good served with this meat.

No. 24—BEEF SALAD.

Quantity for 6 Persons.

1 lb. of boiled beef
2 yolks of eggs
Vinegar to taste
Salt
1 pinch of pepper
1½ tbsps. of oil
½ tsp. of grated onions
2 tsps. of capers
½ cup of cold bouillon
3 tbsps. of cream
½ tsp. of mustard

Preparation: The meat is cut in cubes and mixed with the egg yolks and cream. Now vinegar, bouillon, mustard and all the other ingredients except the oil are mixed in well. After the salad has stood for 1 to 2 hours, covered up well, the oil is stirred in. The salad is served in mound-shape, garnished with hard-boiled eggs and pepper-pickles cut into nice slices.

No. 25—CROQUETTES.

Quantity for 6 Persons.

1 lb. boiled beef
½ lb. raw or boiled chopped pork
¼ onion, grated
2 rolls soaked in water
Salt
1 pinch of pepper
1 tsp. of capers
Juice of ½ lemon
2½ tbsps. of butter or lard
2–3 eggs

Preparation: The meat is chopped fine or ground twice and mixed well with all the given spices and the soaked rolls. Make oblong dumplings of this mass, roll them in roll crumbs and fry to a light brown in the butter or lard. For gravy serve one of sardines or prepare one of the croquette drippings as follows: When the croquettes are done put ½ tablespoonful of flour into the drippings and let it stew a while, then add ½ cup of bouillon or water, ½ teaspoonful of meat extract and salt according to taste. Let it boil a while and pour the gravy over the croquettes.

No. 26—MEAT PUDDING No. 2.

Quantity for 6 Persons.

1 lb. boiled beef or roast beef
⅛ lb. bacon
2 yolks of eggs
2 whites of eggs beaten to foam
4 tbsps. of gravy
½ tsp. of grated onions
1 tsp. ground capers
1 roll soaked and the water pressed out
Salt, pepper
½ tbsp. of butter
1 tbsp. of roll crumbs
3 chopped sardines

Preparation: Meat and bacon are chopped fine and mixed well with yolks of 2 eggs, gravy, chopped sardines, onion, salt, capers, pepper and the roll. Add the beaten whites of eggs; put into a pudding mold which has been buttered and strewn with roll crumbs. Set it in a steamer over a kettle of boiling water and let it steam 1½ hours, or bake in the oven for 1 hour.

No. 27—KÖNIGSBERGER KLOPS.

Meat Balls.

Quantity for 6 Persons.

1½ lbs. finely chopped raw beef

¼ lb. fat pork, chopped
⅛ lb. of butter
1½ roll:—the crust cut off
1 tsp. of grated onion
3 eggs
1 pinch of pepper
Salt
The juice of ¼ of a lemon
Some flour to roll them in

Preparation: The beef and pork are mixed well with the butter; add the roll which has been soaked and the water pressed out, and all other things mentioned above, and mix well. Then small dumplings are made, rolled in flour, and boiled slowly in bouillon or salt water for 15 or 20 minutes. Put them into a deep dish and pour white fricassee gravy over them. Sauerkraut is nice with this meat. You can also fry the Klops instead of boiling them.

No. 28—FRIED BEEF LIVER WITH BREAKFAST BACON.

Quantity for 6 Persons.

2 lbs. of liver cut into thin slices
¾ lb. of bacon cut into thin slices
Salt, pepper, flour

Preparation: The bacon must be lean and is fried light yellow, then placed on a platter on the stove. The liver slices are salted and peppered, dipped into flour and fried in the bacon dripping, quite crisp. It is put on the platter with the bacon. One-half cup of water or bouillon is poured into the lard in which the bacon and liver were fried and left to boil. This gravy may be served separately or on the meat. It requires only a few minutes to fry the liver.

No. 29—COW UDDER.

Quantity for 6 Persons.

1½ lbs. cow udder
1 onion
Salt
2 bay-leaves
1 clove
2 qts. of water
6 pepper-corns

Preparation: The cow udder is washed well and placed over the fire with much cold water. As soon as it comes to a boil the water is poured off and the 2 qts. of fresh water poured on and all the spices named added, then boiled until soft which requires 4 or 5 hours. Then it is cut in pieces, and these are rolled in roll crumbs and fried in butter until light yellow. Or a nice brown gravy is made by taking 2 tablespoonfuls of butter and in it brown 2 tablespoonfuls of flour, then add some of the bouillon, 1 tablespoonful of vinegar, ½ glass red wine, 1 teaspoonful of sugar—all this well cooked.

Now the udder is put into this gravy, stewed a little while and served. The gravy must not be too thick.

No. 30—CORNED BEEF.

30 lbs. of beef
2 lbs. of salt
6 tbsps. of sugar
10 qts. of water
Scant ⅛ lb. of saltpetre

Preparation: Water, saltpetre, sugar and salt are boiled until an egg will float on the mixture. Then this mixture is poured, while hot, on to the fresh meat. The liquid must be 1½ inches above the meat after a stone or something heavy is placed on it. The meat may remain in this mixture for 3 to 4 weeks and should be turned once in a while. Smaller pieces need only 8 to 10 days.

No. 31—CORNED BEEF FOR COOKING.

Quantity for 6 Persons.

3 lbs. of pickled beef
4 qts. of water
Some soup greens

Preparation:. When the beef is very salty, soak it in water for a few hours. Put it to boil with the 4 qts. of water and soup greens and boil for 2½ to 3 hours slowly. Larger pieces need more time.

Cabbage goes nicely with this beef. In carving, cut against the grain.

No. 32—SMOKED CORNED BEEF.

When the meat is taken out of the brine, hang it in a cool, airy place for one day and then smoke it.

No. 33—PICKLED BEEF TONGUE.

2 tongues
¼ lb. of salt
1 tsp. of saltpetre
1 tbsp. of sugar

Preparation: The throat end is cut off and the skin of the tongue is cut with a sharp knife at several places. Salt, sugar and saltpetre are heated and the tongues rubbed well with the mixture. They are then packed into a jar and weighted with a stone. They must be turned every day. It takes 10 to 14 days to pickle the tongues.

No. 34—SMOKED, PICKLED OR FRESH BEEF TONGUE FOR COOKING AND FRYING.

Quantity for 6 Persons.

For Cooking.

1 fresh, smoked or pickled beef tongue
1 bay-leaf
6 pepper-corns
2 cloves
Some soup greens
½ onion
3 qts. of water

For Frying.

2 tbsps. of butter
1 tbsp. of flour
½ cup of bouillon or water
½ wine glass of red wine
½ tsp. of sugar
Juice of ¼ lemon

Preparation: Cut off the throat end and if the pickled tongue is too salty, leave it in water for a few hours, the same with fresh tongue to remove the slime or mucous. The smoked tongue is left in water over night. After this is done the tongue is cooked until soft in the 3 qts. of water, adding bay-leaf, pepper-corns, cloves, soup greens and onion. If it is a fresh tongue, add some salt. It requires 3 hours to cook a tongue.

When the tongue is soft, take it out of the water and skin it. You can serve the tongue in this manner or cold and sliced. If you wish to serve the tongue warm and whole, it is nicer to fry it. Put it into a low frying pan, add the given quantity of butter and fry it 10 minutes on both sides, add 1 tablespoonful of flour and let it simmer a few minutes. Now add the bouillon or water. With the water put in ¼ teaspoonful of meat extract, red wine, sugar, salt and lemon juice, and then cook ¼ of an hour, basting it several times. Then serve. The gravy must be strained.

Boiled, warm tongue is nice with vegetables. Cut the tongue into slices and place it around the vegetables like scales.

No. 35—RAGOUT OF OX-TONGUE.

Quantity for 6 Persons.

For Cooking.

1 tongue, smoked, pickled or fresh
3 qts. of water
2 cloves
6 pepper-corns
¼ onion
1 bay-leaf

Sauce.

3 tbsps. of butter
3 tbsps. of flour
½ qt. bouillon or water
½ cup Madeira or red wine
1 pt. of champignons
6 truffles
Juice of ½ lemon
1 tsp. of sugar
Salt
3 pepper-corns
1 clove
½ bay-leaf
¼ tsp. of meat extract
1 slice of lemon

Preparation: The tongue is cooked the same as in No. 34. For ragouts the smoked tongue is preferable. When the tongue is soft, skin it and cut it into thin slices.

Gravy: Brown the butter and flour, add the bouillon, salt, sugar, pepper, 1 clove, ½ bay-leaf, one slice of lemon and the juice of ½ lemon, Madeira or red wine and the water from the champignons. Let it boil for ½ hour and strain.

Peel the truffles, chop them fine and put them into the strained gravy and if the champignons are large cut them into quarters and put them also in the gravy and finally the slices of tongue. The gravy must not be too spicy if it is a smoked or pickled tongue. After the ragout has been thus prepared it may stew on the stove for ¼ hour. The gravy must not be too thin and watery.

The ragout is placed on a platter and garnished with warm scallops of puff paste or meat dumplings.

Meat Dumplings.

¼ lb. finely chopped veal
¼ lb. finely chopped pork
1 roll, soaked and the water pressed out
Some grated onion, salt, pepper
1 tbsp. of finely chopped champignons
1 tsp. of finely chopped truffles.
1 egg

Mix this all very well and form small dumplings, then put them into boiling hot salt water or bouillon and cook for 10 minutes slowly, or fry in butter light brown and place them around the tongue ragout.

The plates and the platter on which they are served must be hot.

Remarks: This is a fine dish for parties.

No. 36—CHOP SUEY.

For About 6 Persons.

½ lb. veal
½ lb. pork

1 lb. beef
2 tsps. molasses
1 large stalk celery
3 large onions
1 tbsp. lard
1 tbsp. flour

Preparation: Cut the meat in cubes; put the lard and flour in pan and brown; add meat and put enough water on to cover it; add the molasses and cook slowly for 1 hour.

Cut the stalk of celery in small pieces and add them to the meat. Cut the onions fine and fry them light brown in a little butter; add to the rest and boil slowly another half hour. Serve with plain Chinese sauce.

CHAPTER 3.
VEAL.

1. Leg.
2–3. Kidney roast and small chops.
4. Shoulder.
5. Neck.
6. Breast.
7. Head.
8. Shank Leg.
9. Four Legs.

Preparation of Veal.

Appearance of Good Veal.

It must be of a white color, a fine firm grain and have plenty of fat.

Do not buy very young veal because those calves are as a rule not healthy. Cheap meat is never economical. Veal is quickly prepared because it does not require long boiling. The bouillon is good for invalids because it contains much gluten.

Best Pieces for Roast.

Leg or Loin.

The leg with the fricandeau, the fillet, loin and kidney roast.

Small Pieces for Frying.

The chump end of loin for chops, veal cutlets from rib piece, fillet.

Pieces for Pot Roast.

The breast, neck, shoulder.

Pieces for Boiling.

The thick rib piece, neck.

Pieces for Bouillon.

The calves' feet, calf-bones, calf-tail, also lean meat.

Parts for Fricassee.

Lungs, brain, sweetbreads, breast piece.

No. 1—LEG OF VEAL.

Quantity for 8–10 Persons.

6–8 lbs. leg of veal
⅛ lb. of bacon
⅛ lb. of butter
½ cup sweet or sour cream

Salt, pepper
1½ cups of water
2 tbsps. of flour

Preparation: The meat is pounded, boiling water poured over, i.e., scalded, which makes the meat white; let the water run off immediately. Sprinkle with salt and pepper and put into pan. Cut the bacon into thin slices and put it on the meat, add the butter and place into oven. Roast for 2 hours, basting frequently. About ½ hour before done, put the flour into the gravy and stew 5 minutes, then add water and put the cream on the leg in spoonfuls. When the roast is tender, put on platter and strain the gravy which must not be too thin.

Remarks: If the roast has much stock, pour some off before adding flour, stand cold and let it jelly. Now cut it into slices and serve with slices of tenderloin. Veal roast may be utilized in various ways.

No. 2—WARMED UP VEAL ROAST.

Quantity for 6 Persons.

1½ lbs. of veal roast
⅛ lb. of butter
⅛ lb. of sardines
1 tbsp. of capers
Some salt
Juice of ½ lemon
Left over gravy
For the gravy, 1 tsp. of flour

Preparation: Put the roast into an earthen dish, heat the gravy, pour it over the roast, cover up the dish, place it into a covered pot with boiling water, let it boil slowly for one hour and baste the roast several times.

The gravy is usually thin, therefore add the flour and serve with the roast; the contents of the dish must not boil, otherwise the roast will become dry. Cut the roast into slices, place them into a buttered mold, put the sardines, capers and bits of butter between them and drip the lemon juice on. Cover the mold, put it into the dish with boiling water and boil for ¾ hours. The meat is served in the mold, the gravy heated and served with it.

No. 3—VEAL ROAST WITH POTATOES.

Quantity for 6 Persons.

1 lb. of veal roast
Salt
1 pinch of pepper
¼ onion
Left over gravy
4 big, raw potatoes, peeled and cut into thin slices

Preparation: The meat is cut into small pieces, placed in 2 or 3 layers alternately with sliced potatoes into an earthenware buttered dish so that the top layer will be potatoes. Season each layer with salt, pepper and a little onion.

The meat gravy which may be diluted with bouillon or water is poured over the whole until level with the potatoes; then put small pieces of butter on top and bake in the oven for 1½ hours.

If you have no left over gravy then take 1 tablespoonful of butter, brown it, stir in 1½ tablespoonfuls of flour, add water or bouillon, ½ teaspoonful of meat extract, 3 tablespoonfuls of cream (if on hand), boil and pour over the potatoes and meat and bake. Serve in the earthen dish.

No. 4—VEAL ROAST RAGOUT—BROWN.

Quantity for 6 Persons.

1½ lbs. of veal roast
½ pt. brown gravy
1½ tsps. sugar

1¼ tbsps. vinegar, (preferably wine vinegar)
1 tbsp. butter
2 gherkins or 4 sweet-sour pickles
1½ tbsps. of small pearl onions; pickled ones preferred

Preparation: If you have no left over gravy then make a false gravy by directions given in No. 3. Add sugar and vinegar according to taste, cut pickles into small pieces and put into the gravy with the onions. Cut the meat into pieces and put it into the hot gravy; it must not boil, otherwise the meat will be tough; put another piece of butter on top and serve.

No. 5—SHELLS FILLED WITH VEAL ROAST.

Quantity for 6 Persons.

½ lb. veal roast
1½ tbsps. of butter
2 tbsps. of flour
Salt, pinch of pepper
3 tbsps. of white wine
Juice of ½ lemon
½ cup of cream
1 cup of bouillon or water and ¼ tsp. meat extract
½ tbsp. of Parmesan cheese, grated
1 tbsp. of rolls, grated

Preparation: The butter is melted and flour stirred in. Stew it and add water or bouillon (if you take water, use ¼ teaspoonful of meat extract), cream, white wine, salt, pepper, lemon juice. The gravy must boil. Taste it to make sure that it may not be either too salty, too sweet, or too sour.

Chop the veal roast and put it into the gravy. The mixture should be pretty thick; fill it into the shells, sprinkle with the Parmesan cheese and roll crumbs and place small pieces of butter on top. Then bake them in the oven to a light yellow color which requires 10 minutes. Serve at once.

No. 6—VEAL ROAST PUDDING.

Quantity for 6 Persons.

1 lb. veal roast
⅛ part of an onion chopped fine
3 tsps. of parsley, chopped fine
⅛ lb. of butter, good measure
3 eggs
Salt
1 pinch of pepper
¼ cup of sweet cream
1 roll, grated
½ pt. of tomato or sardine gravy
1 tsp. of Parmesan cheese

Preparation: The veal roast is chopped fine. Three-fourths of the butter is creamed, and the 3 yolks stirred in, meat, salt, pepper, Parmesan cheese, roll crumbs, cream, parsley, all well mixed. The chopped onion is cooked in butter for a little while and then stirred in.

The white of egg is beaten stiff and also added to the mass. A tin pudding mold is buttered and strewn with roll crumbs, the mixture put in, and the closed mold set in a steamer over boiling water and steamed for one hour.

Dump the pudding on a hot platter and pour over it tomato or sardine gravy.

No. 7—VEAL ROAST SALAD.

Quantity for 6 Persons.

1 lb. veal roast
3 yolks of eggs
1 tbsp. of flour
2 tsps. of salt
Some pepper

1 tsp. of mustard
¼ qt. of milk
½ tbsp. of butter
4 mustard pickles
2 tbsps. of pearl onions
3 tbsps. of wine vinegar

Preparation: Milk, flour, yolks of eggs, salt, pepper, vinegar, and butter are stirred to a gravy and brought to boil. It requires 10 minutes time till the gravy is thick and smooth. Veal roast and pickles are cut into thin slices. Meat, pickles and onions are put into layers in a dish and between each two layers a few spoonfuls of gravy, concluding with gravy over the top.

Three hard-boiled eggs quartered and placed on or around the salad makes it look nice.

No. 8—SADDLE OF VEAL.

Quantity for 10 Persons.

6–7 lbs. of veal saddle
Some salt
1 pinch of pepper
¼ cup of butter, or good roast drippings
¼ lb. of bacon
1 cup of cream
2½ tbsps. of flour

Preparation: The saddle of veal is well prepared by the butcher so it will lie flat in the pan. Skin and scald the veal and lard it with bacon, then sprinkle with salt and pepper and put into the pan. Heat the butter, pour it over the meat and set it into a medium hot oven. Pour a little water over once in a while so the butter does not get too brown; the roast must be basted every 10 minutes to make it juicy. It requires 1 or 1½ hours roasting to make it tender. One-quarter of an hour before done put in the flour and cream. The gravy must be strained before serving. The kidneys may be removed, cut into thin slices, arranged around the roast with the pieces overlapping each other like scales.

Remarks: The gravy may be prepared in various ways. Instead of cream take ¼ cup of Madeira or red wine and cut truffles into thin slices and put into the gravy.

Another way is to take cream and champignons and lemon juice.

The left over roast may be utilized for ragout, gulash, fricassee, meat dumplings or in a pudding made of roast and potatoes. The bones are split and used to make bouillon.

No. 9—ROAST VEAL LOIN WITH KIDNEY.

Quantity for 6 Persons.

3 lbs. of veal loin with the kidney
Salt
1 pinch of pepper
⅛ lb. of butter or lard
1 tbsp. of flour
¼ cup of cream
½ cup of water

Preparation: Pound the meat and sprinkle with salt and pepper. Cut the kidney off and if it is very fat, cut some of the fat off and render it to be used for frying or cooking. The roast is then put on and basted with hot butter or lard; the kidney is put in with the roast. Let it roast until well done and baste it frequently. Shortly before it is done, add flour to the gravy and then the cream. If there should be too little gravy, add more water and let it roast ¼ hour longer. Baste with the gravy several times and serve. The gravy must be strained, the kidney cut in slices and arranged around the roast for garnishing.

No. 10—ROASTED FRICANDEAU OF VEAL.

Quantity for 6 Persons.

3 lbs. fricandeau or cushion of veal
1 small piece of bacon for larding
⅛ lb. of butter
½ cup of cream
1 cup of water
1 tbsp. of flour

Preparation: The fricandeau, which is a choice piece of lean meat cut from the thickest part of the leg, is nicely trimmed, pounded and larded with bacon. It requires 1 to 1¼ hours to roast it. Prepare it just the same as directed in <u>No. 9</u>.

No. 11—STUFFED BREAST OF VEAL.

Quantity for 6 Persons.

3½ lbs. of breast of veal
⅛ lb. of butter for roasting
Salt, 1 pinch of pepper

The Filling.

½ lb. of chopped beef or veal
½ lb. of chopped pork
1½ soaked rolls
1 tbsp. of butter
¼ tsp. of grated onion
2 eggs
Salt, 1 pinch of pepper
2 tsps. of finely chopped parsley
Juice of ¼ lemon

Preparation: The meat is pounded a little, washed, an incision is made between meat and bone and ¼ teaspoonful of salt rubbed in. The ingredients for the filling are mixed well and put into the cavity formed by the cut, then sewed up. The ⅛ lb. of butter is heated, the stuffed breast put in and roasted a little; then add 2 tablespoonfuls of flour, sprinkle with salt and pepper, let it cook 10 minutes.

Now pour in 1 cup of water, roast for 1½ hours, basting frequently. Strain the gravy and serve.

No. 12—BREAST OF VEAL WITH BEER.

Quantity for 6 Persons.

5 lbs. of breast of veal
Salt
4 pepper-corns
2 cloves
1 bay-leaf
½ small onion
3 thin slices of lemon
3 tbsps. of flour
⅛ lb. of good butter, heaped
1 bottle of beer

Preparation: This breast of veal should be from the brisket end as the meat is thicker and it does not have as much bone and skin as a piece from the middle breast. It must be pounded and tied with a white string into a good shape. Then it is roasted in the butter to a nice brown color on all sides. When this is done, put the meat into another dish. Put the flour and sliced onion into the butter, cook them brown and add the beer; then add all the spices, put in the meat, cover, and bake in oven slowly for 2 hours, turn over occasionally and baste with gravy. If you do not like beer, use water. The gravy must not be too thin; if it gets too thick, add more water or beer; strain it. Garnish the roast with slices of lemon.

No. 13—CALF'S HEAD RAGOUT.

Quantity for 6–8 Persons.

1 calf's head with brain and tongue
½ lb. of beef
½ lb. of veal
¼ lb. of raw ham
6 pepper-corns
2 bay-leaves
1 piece of tarragon
1 piece of carrot
1 piece of celery
1 piece of kohlrabi
½ of tomato
Salt
½ pt. red wine
⅛ lb. of butter
1 onion
⅛ lb. of flour
1 pinch of paprika
¼ pt. of Madeira
Juice of ¼ lemon
1 tsp. of sugar
4 hard-boiled eggs cut into ⅛ths
1 piece of parsley root

Preparation: The calf's head is split in half, the brain and the tongue taken out and soaked in water. Take the skin off the calf's head, brush the skin in water until it is white, then boil it with the tongue until tender. Put in the split head bones, all the soup greens, salt, pepper-corns, bay-leaf, tarragon and boil for 2 hours. The bouillon must be boiled down to 1½ or 2 qts.

When the skin is done, cut it into squares. The tongue is skinned and cut into slices. Both are put into a dish and red wine, salt and pepper added.

Beef, veal, ham and onion are cut into pieces and fried brown in ⅛ lb. of butter. Add ⅛ lb. of flour, cook a little and add the calf's head bouillon and Madeira and cook slowly for 2 hours. The gravy must be strained, the fat taken off and then seasoned. Put into it the pieces of skin and tongue, some lemon juice and sugar. Serve the ragout on a hot platter. Fry the brains to a light yellow, cut it in pieces and garnish the ragout with them; also with scallops of pastry and the ⅛ths of eggs. It is a fine side dish.

No. 14—CALF'S TONGUE.

Quantity for 6 Persons.

3 calves' tongues
Salt
2 qts. of water
6 pepper-corns
1 bay-leaf
2 cloves
1 slice of lemon
¼ onion

The Gravy.

½ cup of sour cream
⅛ lb. of butter
3 tbsps. of flour
2 tbsps. of lemon juice
2 tbsps. of capers
¼ tsp. of sugar
2 yolks of eggs
Salt, 1 pinch of pepper

Preparation: The tongues must be fresh and washed well, cooked until tender in 2 qts. of water with all the given ingredients, then skinned and cut into slices.

The Gravy: Butter is heated, flour stirred in, bouillon added and cooked well with lemon juice, cream, sugar and capers.

The slices of tongue are put in the gravy and heated, the yolks of eggs stirred in and then served. The gravy must not be too thin. The slices of tongue may be salted, dipped into yolks of eggs and roll crumbs and fried in butter.

No. 15—CALF'S BRAINS.

Quantity for 6 Persons.

3 calves' brains
Some salt
1 pinch of pepper
1 egg
½ cup of grated rolls
1 qt. of water

Preparation: The brains are soaked in water. One quart of water is brought to boil, the brains put in and boiled for 5 minutes, then taken out and the small veins and skin removed, then salted and peppered. Beat the egg well, dip the brains in and then in roll crumbs and fry in hot butter to a golden yellow.

Remarks: When the brains have been thus prepared, drip a few drops of lemon juice on and then bake, or, it may be served with lemon slices.

No. 16—VEAL FRICASSEE.

Quantity for 6 Persons.

2½ lbs. breast of veal (brisket)
2 qts. of water
¼ onion
4 pepper-corns
2 cloves
½ bay-leaf
Salt

Gravy.

3 tbsps. of butter
2 tbsps. of flour and bouillon
2 yolks of eggs
1 wineglassful of white wine

Preparation: The meat is cut into nice pieces and the cartilage left on. Scald it for ½ minute and drain well. With the 2 qts. of water, onion, salt and spices, it is boiled until tender. Boil down the bouillon to ¾ of a quart so it is very strong. It requires 1 hour to cook the meat done.

The Gravy.

Heat the butter, put in the flour and stew a little. Butter and flour must remain white, stir in the veal bouillon gradually that the gravy may become smooth. Then add the white wine and cook 1 minute, stir in the yolks of eggs and stop cooking. The meat, which has been kept hot, is put into the gravy and served. Rice cooked in water and bouillon is nice served with this. Place the meat in the middle of the platter and garnish with the rice.

No. 17—VEAL GULASH.

Quantity for 6 Persons.

2¼ lbs. of veal
1 small onion
1 tbsp. of butter
1 pinch of pepper
1 tbsp. of flour
1 cup of water
Salt

Preparation: The meat is cut into 1½ inch squares. The onion is cut into small cubes and fried slightly in the butter, the meat is then added and stewed 10 minutes. Add the flour, salt and pepper and stew 5 minutes more. The water is then poured in and covered up. Stir it once in a while and let it cook until done, which will require about 1½ hours. Gulash must not be too juicy.

No. 18—UNBREADED VEAL CUTLETS.

(Chops).

Quantity for 6 Persons.

3 lbs. veal chops
⅛ lb. of butter
Salt
1 pinch of pepper
½ cup of cream
Juice of ¼ lemon
½ tbsp. of capers
½ tbsp. of meat extract if necessary
1 cup of water

Preparation: The cutlets are cut from the back, each one containing a bone. It is pounded, shaped neatly and sprinkled with salt and pepper. The butter is heated, the cutlets put in and fried brown on both sides, then put on platter. Put into the butter the ½ tablespoonful of flour and brown it. Should there be too much butter, take some out before putting in the flour, then pour into the butter and flour one cup of water, salt if necessary, lemon juice and cream. Press the capers through a sieve and stir into the gravy. Put the cutlets into this gravy, cover the pan and stew 10 minutes, then serve. If the gravy is too light brown, add the ½ teaspoonful of meat extract.

Remarks: Anyone who does not like the taste of capers and lemon juice may leave them out, also the cream. If you wish the gravy very fine, leave off the above and add champignons and finely chopped or cut truffles and 2 tablespoonfuls of Madeira.

No. 19—BREADED VEAL CUTLETS.

3 lbs. of veal cutlets
1 egg
1 tbsp. of milk
Salt, pepper
Roll crumbs, or cracker crumbs
⅛ lb. of butter

Preparation: The cutlets are pounded, shaped neatly and sprinkled with salt and pepper. The egg is mixed well with the milk; in case you have some white of egg left over, use that with milk, dip the cutlets into it, then into the roll or cracker crumbs and place them into the hot butter to brown on both sides. Put the fried cutlets on a platter.

The Gravy: Put ¼ tablespoonful of flour into the hot cutlet butter and stew, add a half cupful of water, cook a little while, pour it over the cutlets, garnish with lemon slices and serve.

No. 20—VEAL CUTLETS AS A FINE SIDE DISH.

Quantity for 6–8 Persons.

3 lbs. of veal cutlets
1 lb. of sweetbreads
½ lb. of boiled calf's tongue
1 pt. can of champignons
Salt, pepper
⅛ lb. of butter
1 tbsp. of Parmesan cheese
1 tbsp. of crab butter
1 small can of truffles

Preparation: The cutlets are pounded, salted and peppered and fried to a light brown on both sides in ⅛ lb. of butter.

The tongue is cooked well done in water with salt, a piece of onion, 4 pepper-corns, 2 cloves, 1 bay-leaf; ¼ hour before done, put in the sweetbreads. When both are done, skin them and chop them or cut them into cubes.

The gravy: Put 2 tablespoonfuls of flour into the cutlet butter, stew a little while, then add bouillon in which the tongue and sweetbreads were cooked, add some of the champignon juice, a wine glass of red wine, 1 tablespoonful of lemon juice, 1 teaspoonful of sugar and cook for ¼ hour, strain and put champignons, finely chopped truffles, sweetbreads and tongue in the sauce and heat.

Put the cutlets into an oblong or round casserole, strew with Parmesan cheese, drip some crab butter over. The ragout is poured over them and the whole is baked in the oven for ¼ hour and when served in the casserole, it is a very fine dish.

No. 21—CHOPPED VEAL CUTLETS.

Quantity for 6 Persons.

3 lbs. of veal cutlets
Salt, pepper
Some flour
⅛ lb. of butter
1–2 eggs

Preparation: The cutlets are chopped and cut off the rib bone. Remove all tendons and skin, and shape the chopped meat round and press it against the bone. Beat the egg well. Salt and pepper the cutlets, dip carefully into the egg and then into the flour. Now heat the butter and fry the cutlets in it to a light brown on both sides. Handle them carefully so they will not fall apart, then take them out and place them on a hot platter. Put ½ cup of water into cutlet butter, salt if necessary and cook, pour over cutlets, garnish with lemon slices and serve.

No. 22—BREADED VEAL CHOPS.

Quantity for 6 Persons.

2¼ lbs. of veal
Salt, pepper
½ tbsp. of flour
1 or 2 whites of egg
1 tbsp. of milk
1 cup of roll or cracker crumbs
⅛ lb. of butter or half butter and half lard
¾ cup of water

Preparation: The meat for this must be from the loin or leg. It is cut into ¾ inch slices, pounded, salted and peppered. Beat the white of egg well or take egg and milk, dip the pieces of veal in and then into the roll or cracker crumbs. Fry them brown in the hot butter or lard, this will require 10 minutes. They must not be rare inside. For the gravy, put ½ tablespoonful of flour into the lard or butter, brown and add ¾ cup of water; add a little salt if necessary, cook well, then pour it over the meat, garnish with lemon slices and serve.

No. 23—VIENNA VEAL-SCHNITZEL, (VEAL CUTLETS).

Quantity for 6 Persons.

2¼ lbs. of veal from the leg
Salt, pepper
2 eggs
Juice of ½ lemon
⅛ lb. of butter
6 eggs
Flour

Preparation: The veal is cut into six ¾ inch thick slices, pounded, salted, peppered. Beat the eggs well, dip the meat into it and then sprinkle with flour. Heat the butter and fry the slices to a light brown on both sides. While they are frying, drip the lemon juice on. When well done, put them on a hot platter. Make the gravy with ½ cup of water poured into frying butter and salt if necessary, cook and pour over the cutlets. The eggs are fried and placed on each cutlet carefully so the yolk does not run out.

No. 24—VEAL CUTLET OR SCHNITZEL A LA HOLSTEIN.

Quantity for 6 Persons.

2¼ lbs. of veal from the leg
2 eggs
Salt
1 pinch of paprika
⅛ lb. of butter
4 hard-boiled eggs
2 tbsps. of pickled beets, chopped
1 tbsp. of capers
1 small pickle
6 sardines
6 slices or six-eighths of a lemon
¼ tbsp. of flour
¾ cup of water
½ tsp. of meat extract
1 tbsp. of onions

Preparation: The meat is cut into six ½ inch thick slices, sprinkled with salt and paprika and dipped into well-beaten egg. The butter is heated and the meat fried brown on both sides, then put on a hot platter. The ¼ tablespoonful of flour stirred into the butter and ¾ cup of water added with ½ teaspoonful of meat extract and salt, if necessary, then boiled and poured over the meat.

The hard-boiled eggs are chopped fine, the whites separate from the yolks. The sardines are drained and cut into halves lengthwise, then rolled up. Now arrange your dish neatly, little heaps of beets, onions, pickle, white and yolk of egg, lemon slices on each cutlet. The rolled sardines in the middle of the lemon slice, heaps of the rest around each and the capers singly in between. Should be prepared quickly but appetizingly.

No. 25—VEAL CUTLETS IN WHITE WINE.

Quantity for 6 Persons.

2½ lbs. of veal from the leg
⅛ lb. of butter
Salt, pepper
1 kohlrabi, cut into dainty pieces
½ carrot, cut into dainty pieces
½ parsley root, cut into dainty pieces
⅛ celery root, cut into dainty pieces
10 small pieces of cauliflower
½ pt. of white wine.
1 cup of water
2 tbsps. of flour.

Preparation: The meat is cut into slices ¾ inch thick, salted and peppered, then fried light brown on both sides in the heated butter and placed on a platter.

For the gravy stir 2 tablespoonfuls of flour into the butter and brown, then add water and wine, the vegetables and salt. The vegetables must be cooked very tender, then put in the veal schnitzel or cutlets and cook slowly for 20 minutes. The whole, schnitzel, gravy, and vegetables, is served in one dish. It makes a fine dish. The gravy must not be thick.

No. 26—VEAL STEAK FROM THE LEG.

Quantity for 6 Persons.

2½ lbs. of veal

⅛ lb. of butter
1 pinch of white pepper
¼ cup of water
Salt

Preparation: The steak must not be cut too thick. Remove the skin from the steak and pound it well, then fry it in the butter on medium fire for ½ hour, turning and basting it several times. Serve it on a hot platter and sprinkle with salt and pepper and put a little fresh butter over the whole.

For the gravy, pour into the frying butter ¼ cup of water, cook well and strain, then serve separately. Garnish the steak with lemon slices.

No. 27—SWEETBREADS.

Quantity for 6 Persons.

2 lbs. of sweetbreads
Salt, pepper
Roll crumbs or cracker crumbs
⅛ lb. of butter
1–2 eggs

Preparation: The sweetbreads are cooked in salt water for 10 minutes, then taken out and skinned. It is then cut lengthwise if it is very thick and sprinkled with salt and pepper. The egg is beaten well and the sweetbreads dipped into that and then into the roll or cracker crumbs. Then it is fried to a golden yellow in the butter. For the gravy, pour a little water into the hot butter and boil, then pour over the sweetbreads. This is a good dish with vegetables.

No. 28—SWEETBREADS IN SHELLS OR OTHER SMALL MOLDS.

Quantity for 6 Persons.

1¼ lbs. of sweetbreads
½ pt. of champignons, scant
3 truffles
½ wine glass of white wine
Salt
1 pinch of pepper
2 tbsps. of butter
2 tbsps. of flour
Some bouillon
½ tbsp. of Parmesan cheese
½ tbsp. of roll crumbs
½ cup of cream
¼ tsp. of meat extract

Preparation: The sweetbreads are boiled in ¾ qts. of salt water until tender, which requires ¼ hour. Take them out, skin them well and cut them into very small pieces. Boil down the bouillon of it to 1½ cups.

The Gravy: Heat the butter and stir in the flour and stew but do not brown it, then add the bouillon, cream, wine, lemon juice and juice of the champignons, salt and pepper and cook until it thickens.

The champignons and truffles are chopped fine and put into the gravy with the sweetbreads. Heat and fill into shells or other small molds, sprinkle with a little Parmesan cheese, a few roll crumbs and a little piece of butter and bake in oven light brown, which requires 10 minutes. This makes a fine side dish.

No. 29—PUFF PASTE PATTIES FILLED WITH SWEETBREAD RAGOUT.

Quantity for 6 Persons.

½ lb. fresh and very cold butter
½ lb. good flour
1 white of egg
¼ pt. of cold water

1 tbsp. of strong brandy
This makes 6 small patties

The Filling.

¾ lbs. of sweetbreads
¼ pt. of champignons
3 truffles
⅓ wine glass of white wine
Juice of ¼ lemon
1½ tbsps. of flour
1 cup bouillon
½ cup of cream
¼ tsp. of meat extract
Salt and 1 pinch of pepper
1½ tbsps. of butter

The Paste.

Preparation: The flour is made into a smooth paste with water, ½ of the egg and brandy, then rolled out. The butter, which must be very hard, is placed on the paste in a chunk, the paste folded around it and then rolled out again. The board and rolling pin must be well covered with flour. This is repeated 4 or 5 times. The last time roll out the paste ¼ inch thick, cut out with a tumbler or cake cutter, then cut narrow strips and fasten them to the edge of the disk by brushing them first with the egg. Set the strips one on top of another until the edge is 1½ inch high, put a small mold in the opening. With a smaller tumbler, cut out the covers. Bake them both light brown or yellow. After cooling off, carefully remove the small mold, fill the patties with the ragout, cover with the baked covers and bake the patties 10 minutes in medium hot oven. Serve at once.

The filling is made like the one in No. 28. For 6 patties cut out 6 bottoms and six covers and use the other paste for strips.

No. 30—CROQUETTES OF SWEETBREADS.

Quantity for 4 Persons.

1 lb. of sweetbreads
½ pt. can champignons
1½ tbsps. of lemon juice
2 yolks of eggs
2 tbsps. of white wine
Salt, pepper
1 egg
Roll crumbs for breading
2 tbsps. of butter
3 tbsps. of flour
1 cup bouillon
¼ cup champignon juice
¼ cup of cream
Good lard for baking

Preparation: The sweetbreads are boiled in salt water until almost done, then skinned and cut into cubes.

The Gravy: Heat the butter and stir in the flour, add 1 cup of bouillon, white wine, lemon juice, cream, champignon juice, salt and pepper, then boil. It must be savory and thick.

The champignons are cut into small pieces and put into the gravy, also the sweetbread cubes. Then stir in the yolks of 2 eggs. Cool it and shape into oblong croquettes. Beat the egg well, dip in the croquettes and then into the roll crumbs. Bake in deep lard to a golden yellow color. If the croquettes are too soft, add more flour. If you want them as a side dish, take only half the quantity given.

Remarks: You can make croquettes from remnants of veal and prepare them much more simply. See No. 31.

No. 31—CROQUETTES FROM VEAL REMNANTS.

Quantity for 6 Persons.

1 lb. of veal
Salt, pepper
1½ tbsps. of lemon juice
2 yolks of eggs
2 tbsps. of butter or drippings
3 tbsps. of flour
1 cup of bouillon or 1 cup of water mixed with ¼ tsp. of meat extract
½ cup of cream
1 egg and roll crumbs for breading
Good lard for baking

Preparation: The meat is cut very fine. The preparation is the same as in No. 30, Sweetbread Croquettes.

No. 32—MEAT BALLS FROM VEAL REMNANTS.

Quantity for 6 Persons.

1½ lbs. of veal
2 eggs
1½ tbsp. of butter
1 tbsp. of lemon juice
1 pinch of nutmeg
1 tsp. of capers
Salt, pepper
Roll crumbs for breading

Preparation: The meat is chopped fine or ground twice and mixed well with the eggs, salt, pepper, lemon juice, capers and nutmeg. It is then formed into oblong shapes, dipped in roll crumbs and baked or fried to a light brown in hot butter or lard, then placed on a platter.

For the gravy put ½ tablespoonful of flour into the butter or drippings, steep and add ¾ cup of water or bouillon or left over gravy. Strain and pour over the meat balls and serve. They are also good served cold.

No. 33—VEAL HASH FROM REMNANTS.

Quantity for 6 Persons.

1 lb. of veal
1 tsp. of chopped onions
Salt, pepper
1½ tbsps. of butter
½ tbsp. of flour
½ cup of cream
Some water if necessary
2 tbsps. of white wine

Preparation: The meat is chopped and put into hot butter with onions. Cook and then add ½ tablespoonful of flour, salt, pepper and cream and boil slowly for 5 minutes. If it gets too thick, add more water or cream and the wine, if you wish. Serve on fresh wheat bread toast. This is a fine breakfast dish.

No. 34—LIVER DUMPLINGS.

Quantity for 6 Persons.

1¼ lbs. of calf liver
¼ lb. of bacon
3 rolls
⅛ lb. of butter, good measure
4 eggs
Salt, pepper
1 pinch of nutmeg
½ onion
3 qts. of salt water or broth for cooking
2 cups of flour

Preparation: The liver and bacon are chopped very fine or ground twice. The rolls are grated and browned in butter. The onions are cut fine and cooked or fried to a light yellow in ½ tablespoonful of butter.

Mix well the crumbs, onion, eggs, salt, pepper, nutmeg, flour, liver and bacon, then cut out dumplings with a floured round wooden ladle as large as a medium-sized potato. The salt water must boil, then put in the dumplings and cook for 10 minutes. Put them in a dish or platter and baste with browned butter in which some roll crumbs or onions are fried.

Try one dumpling first and if it does not stay whole, add more flour.

Sauerkraut will go well with this dish.

No. 35—VEAL OR CALF'S LIVER WITH BREAKFAST BACON.

Quantity for 6 Persons.

2½ lbs. of calf's liver
½ lb. of bacon
Salt
1 pinch of pepper
1 tbsp. of flour
1 onion
1 cup of water
Flour for dipping
1 oz. of butter

Preparation: Liver is cut into ¼ inch strips and bacon in 3x4 inch slices. The bacon is fried light yellow, then put on a platter and kept hot. The liver is sprinkled with salt and pepper, dipped in flour and baked to a light brown in butter or the bacon drippings. Then placed on the same platter with the bacon and served. Stir into the bacon drippings or butter 1 tablespoonful of flour and the sliced onions, boil and add water or bouillon. Strain the gravy and serve.

No. 36—LARDED AND BAKED CALF'S LIVER.

Quantity for 6 Persons.

2½ lbs. of calf's liver in one whole piece
Salt, pepper
⅛ lb. of bacon for larding
¼ lb. of butter
½ pt. of cream
1 tbsp. of flour
1 carrot
1 onion
1 small piece of celery
5 pepper-corns
2 cloves
1 bay-leaf
1 pt. light white wine

Preparation: The white wine, carrot, onion, celery, pepper-corns, cloves, bay-leaf, 1 pinch of salt are covered and boiled slowly for ½ hour.

The liver is skinned, larded, salted and peppered and the cooked wine with contents poured over. Let stand for 10 hours. After that, roast the liver in hot butter in the oven for 30 minutes and baste frequently. During the last 10 minutes, pour the wine in which the liver had been lying over it and boil. Stir in 1 tablespoonful of flour and cream and boil again. The liver is served on a hot platter. The gravy is strained and served separately. Garnish the dish with lemon slices and parsley.